Blood Don't Make Us Family!

~~~~

Ms. Envious

ISBN – 978-0-578-06224-2

Manufactured in the United States of America.
Self-published & edited

For more information regarding special discounts for bulk purchases and other orders,
please contact ms_envious@rocketmail.com or http://stores.lulu.com/msenvious

This work is a memoir. It reflects the author's present recollections of her experiences
over a period of years. Certain names and indentifying characteristics have been changed.
Dialogue and other events have been re-created and conflated to convey the substance of
what was said or what occurred, but are not intended to be a perfect representation.

Blood Don't Make Us Family!

~~~~~

Blood Don't Make Us Family!

~~~~~

I'm dedicating this book to my children Quintelle, Marquezia, Shyderia, and Quadeyr! I love you all!

~~~

Mommy

Contents

~~~~~

The Kick Off

The Kick Off

Where to start... Like most families there is bound to be a bunch of drama along with happy times & sad times I guess that comes along with the territory. Never in my life did I think I was born into a crazy ass family and that is the nicest way I can describe my so-called families, yeah I have more than one. To be honest I have four families total. So it is like I was expected to have a few screwed up individuals somewhere in one of them, but not 98% of them. I know you are probably like girl everybody has an occasional thought of wishing that they could've been born into another family but not like me.

Yeah everybody goes through drama in his or her life from time to time but not to the point where you would wake up and already know how your day is going to turn out or lay in bed dreading to get up. That is how I feel every day the lord feels the need to breath a breathe of air in my body & everyday I ask myself, why me? So I want to invite you into my nightmare as I call my life. I hope to at least touch one person from my book and to allow those who think they know me to have the opportunity to get to know me the real me. I am also going to touch on some things I have learned through out my life that I would like to share to those of you who want to listen. I have been through a lot in my life more than any person I feel should ever have to go through. If you have been through it trust me you were not alone.

For real I need to do a reality show to really show my families how they really look & how really screwed up they really are. To my families I know you all are going to probably hate me or dislike me after reading this book and to be honest I don't give a F@#$ on the real I am so sick and tired of holding back my feelings about all of you! I feel that it is finally time for me to let all of you know how I really feel about you in the most respectful way I possibly can. So continue to hate on me, I am use to it. Continue to act like the assholes you are; I am use to that also. I'm going to still come out on top believe that!!! So I welcome all of my haters & supporters I love you all at the end of the day!

I have another side I never showed to you

A side where everybody is disposable

To me you were never a threat

Cause I can erase history & act like we never met

Young & Restless

Thinking back to when I was just 8 years old... Growing up out Dover Springs was like a mixed movie on the real with a little bit of horror, sex, drugs, drama, and comedy all mixed together. Before then, I remember when I was like 7 years old we lived out Da Peake. I remember one night waking up to my mama crying and the police dusting off the doorframe. I had no idea what had happen but I knew it was something serious because I had never seen mama cry. Later I found out that mama had just experience the worse thing any woman should ever have to experience. A man broke into our home and attacked her while we were asleep in the next room. Needless to say we didn't stay out Da Peake that long. I didn't like living out there anyway. It was so ghetto on the real. Mama moved us back to the Beach about a week later.

We moved out Dover Springs that same year. I like the neighborhood because it was like family out there. Little did I know looks are definitely deceiving. People were fighting, shooting, arguing, and just acting a plum fool at all times of the day and night. There were many times when we had to go and get into the bathtub because them fools outside would be shooting and mama said it was the safest place in the house. Growing up out there was fun on the real also. Everybody knew everybody and the block parties were off the chain. We would all get together and turn the radio on and have a good old time. The police didn't say anything because we weren't bothering anyone. The men would cook on the grill and we would be in the street showing off our dance moves. There was so much food that you would be able to carry some home at the end of the night.

I seen times we would be double dutching and the local knuckle heads were running around shooting at each other telling us to go in the house. We were so hard headed though because we were like "nah yah need to go in the house!" At that age we thought we were invincible. At night our mothers would hit the club and we would throw parties while they were gone. It was crazy because we party all night without any arguments or fights unlike the house parties nowadays. I started babysitting at the age of 10 for my mama home girls. I figure why not I like making money and they liked going out. So it was like a win - win situation for me. You would think I would've been taught about the birds and the bees early especially with the neighborhood we were living in but I guess mama didn't have time for all of that. All she would do is try to scare us by saying if you get pregnant you are not going to live here or I'm going to kill you; something to try to scare us. Crazy as mama was we definitely believed her.

I started watching this one lady (Meme) kids so much I decided to move in with her somewhat. I mean I was over there every night anyway. Meme house was the spot on the real. Everybody was always over there. I learned so much ova there. I was about 12 years old when I smoked my first and last cigarette, that shit almost killed me. I guess I didn't know what I was doing because I immediately started choking and my eyes got all watery. I started drinking around the same time also, Mad Dog 20/20. That was my shit on the real. My mama never knew what I was doing over Meme house shit I don't even think she even cared for real. I hated being at home because my mama and daddy would fuss and fight all the time so I just stayed over Meme house. I just looked at it like my home away from home.

One day I think I was about 11 years old my mama had went to the club as usual and my daddy was keeping an eye on us for the night which was very rare. I had to use the bathroom. I went in and saw my daddy putting a lighter to a soda can and sucking on it. His eyes looked so scary that I just ran in my room and started crying. I didn't know exactly what he was doing but I put two and two together. I had heard around the neighborhood about him copping drugs from the young boys and most of them who were my friends from school. You can only imagine how embarrassed I was. It had got to a point where I would disown him I mean what little girl wants to say my daddy is a crack head. Kids are evil and I didn't want them to be teasing me. I hated my daddy for that. My mama walked in about a hour later and found my daddy in bathroom passed out on the floor. She immediately started snapping calling him more crack heads and son of bitches than a little bit. Needless to say she knew he was on that shit. She grabbed a knife and chased him around the house. He made it out but not before she sliced his back up on his way out.

After that I saw more men in and out of our house than a little bit. I was mad at my daddy but not enough to be calling another man daddy, which is what my sisters had started doing. That shit use to piss me the fuck off because at the end of the day he was still my one and only daddy. My Nana was the only person other than me who always tried to correct my sisters when they did that shit. My mama didn't care for real they were her men and we had to respect them but not call them daddy. They were nice to us and never touched us but I still couldn't bring myself to call them daddy I didn't care how good they were to us. I only had ONE daddy!

My mama was the type of person who liked to party and dress

sexy so I guess that is where I got it from because I love going out clubbing and showing off my sexy ass body. Besides mama use to tell us if you got it show it because you won't have it all your life. As for my daddy I guess you can say I got my smoking weed from him so to speak. I never did any other drug but weed, shit if weed didn't get me high then it wasn't meant for me to get high. Well I'm not going to fully blame them but they did play a role in those decisions I chose by what they exposed to me. I lost my V-Card 9 days before my 14th birthday and ended up pregnant but that is another story. I guess you could say that came from bad parenting or from me trying to be grown before my time, maybe even both. I am the last person to say I had a smooth ride with that because I didn't. My mama forced responsibility on me, I am kind of glad she did that because it is part of the reason I am a somewhat of a good mother. Now as for my sistas they had a easier ride which to me was not fair at all.

I have seen people get shot when I was like 12 in broad daylight; they lived so I guess that is why it didn't affect me as much. I have lost a lot of friends due to violence though. You would think with as much violence there is in the world some of the youth in this family would at least try to fly right but that is like asking a fat person for one of there twinkies, not happening. I have held conversations with my daddy about him having sex with other women behind my mama back. I don't know why he felt the need to confide in me; for real I thought the shit was trifling. He even told me how he even tried to persuade my mama into using Cocaine with him thinking that it would make their marriage and bond stronger but mama wasn't having that shit. Mama looked at it as the ultimate disrespect. And honestly I don't blame her; my Daddy was really tripping he had a sick way of trying to make bonds stronger with his family, lol! I know it's not funny but my daddy really had some issues he needed to work on.

Family Values

Book Definition of Values - values that are held to be traditionally learned or reinforced within a family, such as those of high moral standards and discipline

You would think that with a family as big as mine there would have a lot of family values and morals but this family doesn't seem to have any at all. Well for my grandparents defense I don't think that the values I'm sure my they tried to instill in their children were passed throughout the generations. I know that sounds crazy although it is sad but true. Bottom line with my mama side is that one could never teach what they never learned and one could never learn what they were never taught. Meaning "each one teach one" in the words of Malcolm X; my generation cannot teach the next generation because they were never taught or they were mis-taught better yet. So the sidewalk needs to end with my generation as far as family values and moral standards go for the next generation or they are really going to be chopped and screwed. I think that my mama side has more Chiefs' than Indians. Everybody wants to be in charge but no one wants to follow until they are ready to lead so to speak. They are killing me with that nonsense. My dad's side is just as bad from what I have learned also.

Since Big Papa died there's been nothing but chaos and turmoil. No one has respect for the next person, there isn't any discipline at all, and all moral standards are non-existent. This family is full of the most disloyal and non-trustworthy people I've ever come in contact with. My dad's side is just as dysfunctional from what I have seen and heard. They do have their flaws but they all stick together at the end of the day somewhat. Which is more that I can say for my mama side. With the people on my mama side you never know if they are truly sincere with you because they are always trying to beat you in the head or get over on you so to speak.

Majority of them are known con artist. Like when I was in high school I had opened my first checking account. Shit I felt like I was on top of the world and semi-grown at the same time. It was my first step of being an independent woman in my eyes. I use to hide my check book along with my id and social security card in my dresser bottom just because I didn't want to lose it and I figured no one would bother to look in there. Boy was I wrong. I started receiving letters in the mail from my bank stating that my account had insufficient funds and a bunch of overdraft charges. Needless to say I was confused as hell especially since I hadn't used my checkbook in months. So when I got to the bank they showed me all of the checks that had been written. My heart nearly jumped out of my chest because I immediately notice the handwriting of one of my closest family members who I thought would never do me like that. I was so wrong and hurt at the same time. I haven't looked at that person the same every since then; my trust was violated and it is hard to just over something like that you know.

Needless to say I wasn't the only one in the family to get betrayed like that because a couple of other people in the family including my Nana have also fell victim. My Nana has to hide her purse in her own home because they have stolen so much from her. She can't even enjoy the comforts of her home; she has to lock her bedroom door while she's in the living room, bathroom, or even asleep at night. It even got to the point where she have had to store her food at my home to avoid the plundering of her freezer and the risk of starvation at the hands of her own children. You would think that they would be helping their mother not trying to send her to the poor house. They know this shit wouldn't fly by if Big Papa were still alive and healthy. It's crazy because my Nana does so much for people and to be betrayed like that is so wrong. Trust karma is a bitch and they will et what is coming to them.

The one thing that still bothers me is the fact that they hate on you for trying to succeed in life and pray on your down fall. Like when I decided to go back to school no one would give me a ride or even watch my children for a couple of hours so I had to drop out. I didn't understand why I could see if I was going out getting in trouble but that was something I never did. My parents can honestly say I was never a problem child but you would think that they would be more than willing to help me especially with all that I have accomplished in my life, but not my family. I don't understand why they don't want to see you become successful or to even have more than what they had growing up. Its like they are always in competition with each other for some reason.

My dad's side well I can't say too much about them because I didn't grow up around them. All I can say is that they stay getting into trouble but they will look out for you if they know that you are family. They are not as self-centered as my mama side from what I have seen but I may be wrong. They do have their flaws but I cannot honestly comment on that because I do not know anything about them like that. I wish it wasn't like that but that's how it is.

Bittersweet Memories

I remember when I was about 7 years old I wanted to go to my cousin Karey's birthday party. I called my daddy because I wanted to wear a new outfit. He came over and brought me this yellow skirt set. It was so pretty. My mama did my hair up all pretty and I had on these fly ass yellow and white boots with some white ruffle socks. You couldn't tell me anything I thought my daddy was the best daddy in the world. He use to always try to make us feel like princesses. Like one time my mama had left and went to the club, I believe I was about 9 or 10 years old. My daddy asked us if we wanted to build a water park in the house. So you know we were like 'damn right'. I think that was the most fun we had with our daddy period. That was until the drill lady came home, mama, she shut down the whole thing. We were mad at her for like a whole week for that. We had a water slide in the dining room, little obstacles throughout the rest of the house, and a mini pool in the bathroom. Lol! We were having so much fun and daddy paid for that because mama snapped, lol!

I also remember and miss when my daddy use to dance with us. He would call us his little princesses and treat like we were at a Royal Ball. We would get all dressed up in our church dresses and meet him in the living room (our Royal Dance Floor). I don't recall mama ever attending any of them though. We had to stand on his feet because we were so short. He also use to let us workout with him all the time. We just looked at it as play time with daddy so we would jump on him and stand on his back while he did push-ups and sit-ups. He didn't mind at all. After daddy left I remember mama use to let us throw parties every Friday. I guess it was her way of bonding with us since daddy wasn't around. Everybody use to come through and she would cook her famous fried chicken. My Nana even told me about how my daddy use to make sure we stayed dressed in the best name brands and furs. Mama, however, was dealing with some demons herself so she would throw them back at him.

I didn't understand then but I do now. She looked at it as his way to make up for going out making children behind her back. My daddy had 3 other children in questioning outside of us. I remember when I was about 3 or 4 my daddy took me over his mama house. He uses to take me over there all the time to see my little brother. He was just a baby but I still loved him. I use to tell my mama about him but she thought I was just talking crazy. I guess with me saying it so often she did some research herself and found out that I was telling the truth. I think she was more hurt than mad because she had always wanted a son of her own and my daddy couldn't give her one but gave another woman one. My dad told me once I was older that mama and him was suppose to raise my brother together because his real mama left him but she came back to get him. It had got to a point where I forgot how my brother even looked. With mama steady telling me I didn't have a brother didn't help much at all because then I started thinking I didn't have one but deep down I knew I did and that he was out there somewhere but I didn't know where and daddy was no help because he either didn't know or didn't want to tell us.

It took 23 years but we found him. Although we wanted to spend years catching up on lost time we are grateful for the time we did get to spend with him even though it was only a couple of months. I can tell you this he was a real man and dedicated father who loved his baby girl dearly. He was a member of the Armed Forces and very athletic. The funny part is that we all clicked automatically it was like we had known each the whole time. The sad part is that we were only 5 minutes away from each all these years and never knew it. The day our brother was taken from us by the hands of some nothing ass niggas was like the worst day of our lives. We had just seen him the day before and we were planning how we were going to spend the summer letting our kids get to know him and his daughter as well as each other. He met all but his oldest nephew who really wanted to meet him. My brother was the type of person who didn't play when it came to his family. Having to grow up too fast he was pushed to raise his younger brother and sister on his mother side. I remember one time we were leaving the mall and I was on the phone with this guy and he had got smart with me and my brother somehow overheard him. He snapped immediately and was like "who in the hell is you talking to like that? Nigga I'll fuck you up on the real don't be talking to my got damn sister like that!" Sometimes he forgot that I was the oldest but it was all good. We loved our brother dearly and still do not understand how someone could just take his life like that. We know that he is watching over us so we when we look up to the sky we just smile because we know he said something to make us laugh.

Do As I Say Not As I Do

Do As I Say Not As I Do

Isn't it funny that the same parenting tactics that you hated as a child are subconsciously being used on your own children? Such as do as I say not as I do. I use to hate it when mama would always say, "Do as I say not as I do." That shit use to piss me off so bad. She only said it when she wanted to have an excuse for allowing us to hear or see something fucked up that she did or said. I remember one time I think I was about 12 or 13. My mom and dad use to fight all the time and she had these home girls who use to come over on a daily basis talking about how their boyfriends use to hit on them. I was confused because they were laughing and joking like the shit was cool and I remember thinking they can't be serious. How could you let another person hit on you and turn right around and laugh about it? I remember one day my boyfriend, at that time, had got smart with me and smacked me in the face. I immediately snapped and went to his ass. When I told my mama about it she got mad and was snapping but when I was like "you didn't act like that when Tammy told you about Chris hitting her or when you was telling them about daddy hitting on you." All she said was what she had always said when she knew she had done or said some fucked up shit around us "Do as I say not as I do." I remember telling myself from that day that I would never be like them when I grew up. I wish a man would put their hands on me! My daddy never hit on me so I'll be damn if any man ever put their hands on me.

One thing that really confused me is all of my mama kids smoke but she act as we were disrespecting her by smoking around her, cigarettes or black and mild's mind you. But she acts as if she wants to be our friend without the benefits of friendship. I could see if we were smoking weed then yeah that would be very disrespectful. But come on she smoke cigs her damn self. Not to mention we are all over 21. She really gets offended when my sistas smoke around her but get this she doesn't say anything about her nieces and nephews smoking around her and she smokes in front of her mama's house, funny I know. I just don't understand that shit for real. Isn't that the pot calling the kettle black? At first she had a problem with us drinking around her that was until one of her boyfriend was like "they are grown what do you mean?" Her rebuttal was "my kids are not going to disrespect me." I don't know if it is just me but that shit sounded stupid as hell especially when she would invite us over to have drinks and play cards. We use to be like "nah for what we can't drink around you remember." The shit that really bothers me is that she doesn't have a problem asking us to help support her habits though. The apple doesn't fall too far from the tree. She knows we all drink and smoke but the issue is us actually doing it. I don't do it around her but if I wanted to she would have a problem. It's a good thing I stopped smoking though.

Oh lets not forget the topic of profanity... she can curse around and at our kids all day but let us do it then it becomes a major problem. That just seems crazy to me. Even when we are having a conversation among each other or with our friends and one of us happens to say a curse word we all of a sudden became disrespectful because she heard it. But my cousins can curse, smoke, and drink around and with her all day and nothing is said. I don't understand but I guess that is where that do as I say not as I do come in. My mama is crazy for real but she can't help it look at the cloth she was cut from. My dad is more laid back, he doesn't mind either way as long as we are not directly disrespecting him. I remember growing up she use to tell us that respect is earned not given and respect those that respect you.

She also would to say how she didn't mind us speaking our mind as long as we were not being disrespectful, yeah right. The same lesson I instill in my children. But when my auntie cursed my son out like he was a grown ass man behind some foolishness that her granddaughter started and he snapped back on her all of a sudden he was being disrespectful. But if it had been someone in the street that did the same thing to him it would have been all right for him to react that way. I don't think so. The way I see it she had no right to talk to him that way she disrespected him and me. Besides if it was that big of an issue she should have came to me not him he was just a child. True my son shouldn't have cursed at her; he could've found another way to react to the whole thing but this family makes act out of character at times. I'm not excusing what he did because he was wrong but so was my auntie. I know myself I get to points where I want to curse everyone in my family out but I just bottle it up and try to move on. I know that I shouldn't do that but I just don't want to add any more fuel to the fire. I know one day I am going to snap because I can feel it. No one sees my point though; I just don't understand this family at all.

Regrets

There are a lot of things that I have regrets about that I have done through out my life that my family had a lot to do with. I am mad at myself for allowing them to take me to the point where I will literally drown myself ova time. I can recall one time when I was 7 in the elementary school I told my peoples I wanted to be famous. They just laughed at me and were like "girl get real you will never be famous." From that day forth I tried to keep believing I would but ova time I started thinking damn they were right. I remember when I graduated from High School I didn't know if I should be happy or not I mean it's hard to feel good about accomplishing something in this family because they make you feel like shit when you do. The only people who came were my mama, my son, and my 2 sistas. My Nana was too sick to attend but it was ok. I remember my son yelling my name from the audience, lol. I only got $40 and that was from my Papa. All of my friends were so happy and planning to go off to college but not me.

I mean who was going to pay for it besides I had a lil boy and a baby on the way not to mention I was basically raising my nephew since his mama really didn't want him; she cared more about running the damn streets. I wonder where she got that shit from, Ma and Dad?

Eventually I went to a local technical school to get a quick trade. That was a total failure because no one would hire me because I didn't have any hands-on experience, sucks I know a waste of $10,000. My sisters dropped out of high school but before they did my peoples would tell them if they graduated from high school they would buy them a car or other shit. Needless to say I was never offered that same deal I guess they knew I would do my best to get all of that. Even when I graduated with my Medical Assistant and Nursing Degree I still didn't get anything. I guess you can say I was really reaching out for some appreciation or for someone to tell me how proud they were of me but I never heard them words no matter how hard I tried. I didn't and still don't understand why.

My biggest regret is having my first child so young. I never had a child hood so to speak. Just because I had a baby so young my mama friends felt as if they could say anything to me as if I was one of them and my mama never corrected them, which was odd to me. My oldest son is really off the chain. I honestly believe if I would've had him at an older age I would have more control of him not to mention my mama and Nana took him from me when he was 9 months old and didn't allow his daddy to be involved in his life. I hate myself for not stepping up to them and saying some back then but I thought I had no choice and that they were just looking out for me and my baby but now I see that they were just being hateful and selfish. I believe that if his daddy would've been allowed to be in his life from the start my son would not be as bad as he is right now. I am just so mad I didn't realize it until it was too late and my son is now an out of control teen. I blame myself for that shit.

The only time I was happy in my teen years was when I was drinking or getting high and dancing because I didn't feel the pain I was trying to conceal. My heart has always been heavy. Sometimes I wish I had a better role model because the men I choose were not good for me; all they did was leave me with a child. I was so stuck on finding love since my daddy was barely there that I started messing with men that I knew were no good. Now I have 4 children with no help.

Another one of my biggest regrets is putting my heart into one person. I use stalk this man and all. I was so in love with him that I didn't see that he was just using me and playing me the whole time. You can only imagine how hurt I was when I found out and I was pregnant for the second time with his child, I had lost the first one. I thought by having his baby that he would love me just as much as I loved him but I was so wrong. The more I tried to give my heart to him the more he played with it. So I called myself getting back at him but ended up pregnant by someone else and he acted as if I had committed the ultimate crime. All of the shit he had done to me he basically acted as if it was nothing. I was even ready to abort my baby just to be with him. Yeah I love this man entirely too much. Looking at my lil man now I cry because I can't believe almost killed him just to be with a man who never really appreciated me from the beginning. The bad part is that I still love this man and I don't know why.

My last regret is getting married so quickly. I should've listen to my gut and waited because I really was not ready to take that big step but I felt as if I had to in order to keep him. Now I see I was stupid as hell for thinking that but at that time I really needed him and I was scared he was going to leave me. After we got married he even told me that he would've left me if I would've said I wasn't ready at that whack ass wedding we had. I wasn't ready at all for that day and every since then we have had nothing but bad luck on the real. I do love my husband but not as much as I really should or as much as he claims to love me. Sometimes I just think about saying forget and start over with him from scratch but he is not with it. Sometimes I think that I put too much emphasis on my wedding day that I can't allow my marriage to work like it should.

I guess you can say I needed a man in my life back then but now I really don't even care if I have one or not. Doing me is working for now. Maybe one day I will either start over with my husband or find someone else. Trust I am going to let him find me this time, I'm done looking.

Pain in my Veins

Pain in my Veins

I have so much pain in my veins because of all of the stuff that I have going on in my head and my heart. I love my family and my husband more than I realized. My family at times makes me feel like I need to be in another family. I mean the shit they do and say is like "what the fuck!" I don't understand them at all or their way of thinking. They call me Booshi' all the time and at first I was offended but now I am like so fucking what it's nothing wrong with loving and wanting more for yourself and your children, which is how I am. They even call my girls Booshi' now but I just laugh at that. My family has hurt me in so many ways ova the years that I don't understand why I still associate myself with them. For example my moms side is so racist that it is sad to even say. I have and had plenty of friend that were not black but I never stayed in touch with them or even hung out with them or invited them ova because I knew how rude my family can be. They would make them feel so uncomfortable and I didn't want to loose any friendship that way.

When I had my oldest child my uncle use to call him a mutt all the time and I would get so angry and start snapping and all my Nana would say is "that is your uncle you are not suppose to talk to him like that". I was so pissed with her too because I was like I am not about to let anyone refer to my baby as a fucking dog. My son was not even mixed he just looked mixed. That is how ignorant my uncle was. There was this other time when my auntie called me in the house because she had heard that I liked and was dating this white boy who stayed out her neighborhood and she poured some salt and pepper on the table and was like you see how that don't mix. I was so offended because Jay was nice and never disrespected me in any kind of way. They never gave him a chance. Needless to say we didn't last long and for real I regret that because he was so good to me. We use to have so much fun together never sexual just kid fun you know.

My family use to and still do talk that racist talk and I still get so pissed because I don't want my children growing up thinking that all white people are evil because there are just as many Black people if not more that are just as evil as White people to their own race. Shit look at the news. We are killing each other on a daily basis ova stupid shit. I have so many mixed family members on my dad's side that it is crazy. It is sad because some of my cousins and my nephews are now starting to talk that same stupid racist shit. I try to correct my nephews; as much as I can but with them steady being subjected to it is really hard.

I have only one main fear that scares the hell out of me and that's receiving that phone call telling me that my oldest son is either in jail, hurt or dead. He is so reckless and hardheaded. He doesn't listen to anyone and I am so scared that he is going to get killed before he turns 18 and he is only 15. My veins hurt so bad when he comes home late or when I hear that he has gotten into a fight weeks after it has happened. Grown men have even tried to get at him. Nowadays kids don't fight they are so quick to pick up a gun and I tried telling my son but he doesn't seem to want to listen. My family isn't any better with helping me with him because they just make it seem like it's my fault that he is the way he is. When they are the ones who had my hands tied from day one. They tricked me into giving up custody to them when he was like 9 months old, telling me if I didn't his daddy would come and take him and there wouldn't be anything I could do about it. I got him back when he was like 4 years old but not legally he just came to live with me but they still had custody of him. When I tried to get him counseling they turned their nose up at me talking about "that's that white folks shit." I felt like if they would've helped me with him instead of trying to undermine me all the time then I wouldn't have to go as far as getting a counselor involved for something they help to create.

One time my husband called himself punishing my son and my peoples acted as if he was literally trying to kill my son. All he did was take his new shoes and clothes from him and told him until he got his shit together he had to wear his old stuff. They even told my son that he didn't have to listen to my husband because he was not his real daddy. Now my husband barely assists me with disciplining him, which pisses me off on the real. My husband is crazy because the last time I checked he is the only one who was helping me take care of my children so he should've stood up to them but he didn't I had to. I wish he would have because maybe my son wouldn't be this way now. Another thing that pisses me off with my husband is the fact that he would know shit about my son and wouldn't tell me until late or until I address the situation. My sister is the same way with not telling me certain shit. I would have to hear about it in the streets or during a conversation that somebody is having. I am so mad at both of them because anything could happen to my child and I would be in the fucking dark about the shit. I would never do anything like that to them. They just don't understand how bad that shit hurts my heart and scares the hell out of me.

What Part of the Game is that?

What part of the Game is that?

My oldest son is a hand full on the real. He is only 15 and thinks he is 18 going on 25. He leaves and come back when he gets ready. He is so disrespectful that none of the adults in the family deal with him. The school officials nor the Law or his father will help me with him. Asking my family for help is definitely out of the question. I am more mad at myself for allowing him to get this fair even though it is not all of my fault I still accept the blame. He went to a party one night with his older girl cousin and they were smoking and drinking. Her daddy went looking for them. He beat her lil ass but my son wouldn't go with him. The guys my son was with pulled their guns out and told him to bounce. Technically that was wrong and my son should've just gone with him but he is so fucking hard headed. So a couple of days later my cousin came into my house and beat the hell out of my son.

At the time I didn't know exactly what was going on. All I knew was what my cousin had told me; which was my son almost got shot because niggas were shooting at the party. I found out later that the nigga that was shooting was someone that my cousin knew; he had the guy shoot in the air to scare the kids. To me that was so fucking stupid because doing bullshit like that only causes them to do the same thing. So technically he put my son in danger by doing that stupid ass shit. His intentions may have been good but he went about it in the wrong manner. I am so mad at myself for that because if I had known all of the details before then I would've tried to stop my cousin. I probably wouldn't have been able to fully succeed but at least I would've tried. I know my cousin didn't intend on really hurting him but he somewhat did.

To make the situation worse, my girl cousin had the nerve to pick my son up and then try to play me like she didn't know where he was the whole time. Acting all concerned and shit when she had him the whole fucking time. I ended up calling the police and listing my son as a runaway because her simple ass didn't tell me she had him with her. Which could've avoided a phone call to the police. After about two days my daddy was like "go check and see if he is over there," talking about my cousin house. When I got around there she I seen my son getting in the vehicle with her, her brother, and her supposed to be boyfriend. Then she had the nerve to break bad as she was pulling off with my son in the car with her.

So we followed her all the way to my Nana's house. She is so petty; she had all that mouth but goes running to my Nana house like a little bitch! When I talked to my son he told me that she wouldn't let him use the phone. Stupid Bitch, that's called kidnapping and abduction. What kills me is she doesn't even take care of her own got damn children but trying to play Super Saver Hoe to my damn son. This is not the first time this twisted ass bitch tried to kidnap my son. When he was about 2 years old she tried to take him then. She was so obsessed with his daddy that she tried to have a baby by him but couldn't so she tried to take my baby. She is a sick as Bitch on the real! She reminds me of one of those damn Lifetime Bitches! All I want to know is what part of the game is that? Seriously! Recently really got me like whoa! My daddy told me that he didn't want any kids and that he wanted my mama to abort me. He said my mama waited for him to go to work and went to my Nana so he wouldn't be able to take her. Thank you mama! Tell me this, should I be mad and hold some type of grudge or should I just let it go? I mean this man basically told me that I ruined his life because I was born. He had such high hopes and big plans; you know what daddy fuck your plans! I'm here and you can either get over it or let me go all together because either way I do not really care. Really, is that something that you should tell your child just because you chose to not still try to be someone in life? I mean look at me I did it and I am still doing it. Just because

I had my children does not mean my life ended, to be honest that was when my life really began. I knew that I had to do something because I didn't want them to have to grow up wanting or wishing for anything and to know that everyone has an opportunity to be whoever it is they want to be in life.

Having my children was the best to that ever happened to me and I wouldn't trade them for anything in the world. I am somewhat still upset that my daddy doesn't feel the same way about his children but that is something that he is going to have to live with. I sat up all night after our conversation crying thinking that I was a bad person and that I ruined someone else life just by existing. Yeah daddy that is how you made me feel. All I want to know is what part of the game is that? Seriously! I went to church about two weeks later and the preacher said something that I had been saying that I was going to do for months... he said there are some people in your life that you do not need and that you need to cut them off. So that is what I am doing I am letting go of all of you who have brought me pain and negativity and that I have brought any pain or regrets to whether it was intentional or not, you all are free of me and I am now free of you, thanks.

Dance like nobody's watching.
Live your life.
Speak your mind like nobody's listening.
It's your life!

~~~~

Love Left

After going through all that I have been through my heart and soul became cold and all the love I had in my heart was gone except for the love I have for my children of course. I have always felt alone and scared even though I had my family and friends around me all the time but I needed more than just that. I needed some companionship and love and my family was not the type to hand that out but they sure knew how to hand out criticism and pain all at the same time. I didn't realize it at first but I have always starved for attention even as a little girl. I now believe that is the reason I chose the situations and men I did. There was a time where I had shut down so far that my mind went completely blank. I have even tried to commit suicide twice behind two men that I was in love with when I was a teenager.

I have been raped 3 times as a teenager and every time I blamed myself because I should've just stayed home with my family but I didn't like to be around them. The first time I felt like I had to give in so that I could go home. But after being raped the second time I just gave up on life. I was more hurt when it happened because my peoples didn't bother to help me and they were right there watching from the next room on a video camera. I had such low self-esteem that I started stripping and doing private parties. I was drinking and smoking weed like crazy. I would have to in order to do the parties. I loved the money but I hated lying to my mom and looking in my son's face not knowing if that was going to be the last time I would see him because the lifestyle I was living was so dangerous. Being young and making as much money as I was making threw that thought right out the window so I kept on doing it. I was staying in some really nice hotels, driving some nice ass rental cars, and my son and nephew was well taken care of so what more could I ask for. I was living the best life I thought was out there. Then I hooked up with my last rapist a guy who I thought I was in love with. He was soooo fine and all the girls wanted him. He had the most sexiest eyes ever and a smile that would drive you crazy. He was crazy though because he use to stalk me all the time. I tried so many times to leave him but every time I tried he would do something to make me think he was trying to change. He was very controlling too. I remember one day I didn't feel like getting down with him so he just took it as if I was a nothing ass bitch in the street. Not to mention I was pregnant by him but after that night I had a miscarriage. I ended up pregnant again not even 2 months later but not by him.

I even told myself that God was just testing me to see how strong I really was and giving me a way out of the situation I was in. I guess I am stronger than I thought. God is so good. I stopped stripping and doing private parties after I got pregnant that time because I was telling myself that this baby really was suppose to be here since I got pregnant again so quick. I just wish I had the guts to tell the truth to my baby father because now he doesn't even know he has a child all because I was scared of my boyfriend at the time, the same man who had raped me. I had gone to him for comfort and one thing led to another and I ended up pregnant. My boyfriend wasn't having that shit though because he physically let me know along with threatening me with his gun. I remember him telling me "I'll kill that nigga for real yo this my baby. If you have an abortion or a miscarriage I'm going to kill you too." I was scared as hell of him when I was pregnant. I had no other choice but to tell my real baby father that he was not the daddy. That was the hardest thing I ever had to do in my life. I haven't seen my baby father since then except when I look in my child's face. I tried looking for him but I haven't had any luck. I cannot even remember his last name. One time he even told me that he had to be the father because he had sex with me all the time and I eventually started thinking the same thing because I only had sex with the other guy twice. That thought went out the window when my DNA test came back.

I tried getting my life back and loving again but for what. There are so many fake ass men out there and I have the bad luck of choosing the wrong ones all the time. I don't know if I have dummy written across my forehead in invisible ink or what. They put on such a good as front that I loose myself in them until it is too late and either I am pregnant, married, or stuck with them. I am just so tired of all of these fake ass niggas on the real I will be so glad when I can find someone who is really sincere you know. Someone who really loves me for me and not for what they can get out of me or what I can do for them. Someone who is true.

Homeless

Homeless

It's funny how family change when you need them. When I got my first apartment you should've seen how quick my sistas packed their shit to move in with me. Being the person I am, I let them come with me. One of them came back twice. The second time she brought her boo with her and I still let them stay. Now that I am homeless with my kids you would think that at least one of their doors would've been offered to me and mines but yeah right. I'm not truly mad at them like I really should be because I know I put myself in this situation this time. I have to give one of them credit because she was and still is willing to put a crib in her name for me. I just have to find one that I can afford and a permanent job. This is my second time being homeless. The first time I lost my crib because I took the blame for everything that happen with this lady that kept fucking with my son. My sistas and I along with the kids in the neighborhood beat the lady up.

Needless to say I had to move after that. Back to Nana's

49

house aka Hell House. There I shared a room with my four children that was no bigger than a master's bathroom. We lived like that for about two years. I even moved into a shelter because I was so stressed at my Nana's house. I went back which was a big ass mistake but I could only live in the shelter for 45 days and my credit was not good enough to get my own place. I even lost custody of my oldest child to his daddy. At the time I felt like he had ripped my heart out I mean I had just lost my crib and here he go taking my child from me. He really tricked me though because we were still sleeping with each other and all, then one day I get a subpoena to go to court. Now I wish I wouldn't have taken my son back from him because now I cannot control him. When he was with his daddy he was doing so good. But I let my family talk me into taking him back again.

Then I started dating this guy who was in somewhat the same situation I was in, living with his family that he didn't want to live with any longer. After six months of dating we moved into an apartment together. He even asked me to marry him. Everything was going so good and was happening so fast and I didn't want to go back to my Nana's house, I made myself believe I was in love with this man. Knowing my heart was not fully in it I still married him only 5 months after moving in with him. I know I was wrong but I figure eventually I would get over my baby father and fall in love with him. I don't even want to get into that day because that was a total disaster all together. I had a lot of faith in him though. We lived in the apartment for a year then we moved into a townhouse. Before we moved into the townhouse I had gotten my section 8 voucher. With my credit being all jacked up I didn't think I was going to be able to get a crib because even though I had section 8 everybody that I went to did credit checks and I didn't have money to keep throwing away on credit checks just to get denied. So we moved into the townhouse and really that is where all of our problems came in.

I wanted a divorce and everything. We were somewhat struggling. Then I found someone to accept my voucher without a credit check. When I told my husband about it he was unresponsive. Before then I had asked him to ask our current landlord at the time if I could use my voucher for the place we were in since it was in just his name but he didn't. I didn't want to loose my voucher so I took the condo. We went from paying $1200 a month to $281 a month. He didn't even help me move our stuff at all. Needless to say I lost a $400 china cabinet and a brand new washing machine because he wouldn't help me move it. I think we were in the condo for about 4 months when he came up with the idea to leave the state and start over. I was all for starting over because I wanted to make my marriage work and I knew my family was waiting for us to break up and I knew a lot of his peoples was probably thinking the same thing.

He had a plan and the money to make the move. You can say I put all my trust in him. I gave up my section 8 like a damn dummy. I really do not think he even wanted me to have section 8 as if he was better than that. Well, we moved to Georgia for like three months and ended up having to move back to Virginia because the economy had went down. We were really struggling down there. I had to call for my family to send us money for food and gas. Neither one of us could find a job out there. Then the car started to act up so we were really out back on the real. We ended up coming back to Virginia and I had to move in with my family and he went back to living with his family again. Just like we started out, crazy huh. The shit that pissed me off was my family had a problem with him catching a ride back with me. I just couldn't believe they acted like that. It's been over a year and I am still staying back and forth from my Nana's to my mama house.

Now the same people that wanted me to come back are the same people who do not want us in their house. Especially my Nana she always telling people how she is going to sell the house and how she will be glad when she has an empty house. Even when my sister moved out my Nana gave that room which was way bigger than the one I was in to my uncle who was never there.

When she did that I knew then that she really didn't want us there. My sister moved out over 2 months ago and that room is still empty. I wish I would've just stayed in Georgia and struggled instead of putting up with this shit everyday. My kids had broken out so fucking badly from the nets in that house. I stop putting food in the house because every time I turned around she was giving it to her grown ass sons like they couldn't go out a get a damn job. I am not obligated to take care of no grown ass man. She would tell everybody I don't put food in the house like I really care. I mean what do I look like a damn fool or something.

Sometimes I just feel like living in my car with my children on the real than to put up with this shit. As for my mama, she was never home so I asked her if my children and I could stay at her house but she was like nah. So that just told me that she didn't care about us either. Her reason is because she didn't want my husband in her house and that she likes to go home sometime which didn't make any sense to me at all. For real that was a dumb ass reason because my husband wasn't going to be over there. Even my god sister was like that was fucked up. She had asked her about me coming there before I did. You would think that my husband had just committed a fucking massacre on the real. I barely even see him on the real. For real sometimes I don't even feel like I am married any longer. Living with this family I believe that I will always be homeless and without. Every time I turn around they always got their hands out for something. I am so tired of being used.

They didn't even want my children there while I went to school or work. I can't even try to better myself within this family. It's not like I am trying to be better than anyone. I just want to show my children that anything is possible if they try hard and stay positive. It's so hard to stay positive or to even keep my children from falling for their negativity with me always at work or school. I don't want to stop going to school or work because then I really will be stuck with them. So I am working my ass off to get up out of this hole they are trying to keep me in. It just seems like every time I see myself getting a few steps ahead something always come up to knock me back even further. I just keep telling myself that I will get through this with or without help from anyone. I just hope that my kids can find a way to forgive me for all that I have put them through.

Is It Possible?

Before I met my second daughter's father I had given up on having a deceit family and love. He was like a dream come true. His family welcomed my children and I with open arms. They made us feel like family from day one and have had ever since then. It's going on 11 years and they have not changed. Even with me getting married and having another baby by someone other than my baby father. They have always kept it real with me and have never cut any corners with me unlike my family. They show that they actually care about my future and the future and well being of all of my children not just the one that I have by their son. To me that was a whole lot more than anyone in my family has ever done for me. What is so crazy is they are more willing to help my children and me without wanting something in return, unlike my own family. When they do stuff for me and mines my family have the nerve to talk junk about them.

One time they took my children to King's Dominion just to

take them and to give me a break. My family acted as if they were trying to be funny just because they took my children to a fucking theme park, crazy right. My family would be like they think they are better than us. I just laughed because they are so petty and childish on the real. I did feel like they were somewhat better than my family, I mean even a blind man could see that. They are not perfect but who is. They treat me like a family should treat anyone in their family. We have had our occasional falling outs, nothing major though. Sometimes they can get on my last nerve and even drive me semi-crazy but I know they mean well. Its like every time I talk to them they always ask how I am doing in school and telling me about different programs that I can do to better myself for my children. For real that is so special to me. I mean to know that someone actually really care about my future makes me feel so appreciated and loved. The only thing that bothers me is when they try to act as if their son is so perfect and put him on this high ass pedestal like he is a saint or something. Little do they know he is not. I still love them though.

My husband's family is just as nice also. They too also welcomed us with open arms. They are always willing to help us when we need it or not. The only thing about them is that they are kind of distant so to speak. I don't think they really ever had a real family or a big family so to speak. I mean my family is huge and I don't think they ever dealt with anyone with a family as big as mine. My mother-n-law is very pushy but you got to love her. She doesn't have any grandchildren except for mines. So she would get upset when they do not want to stay over her house but she needs to understand that she cannot force them to want to be around her. They have to get use to her. Besides they are so use to going over their other grandparent's house. I do not force them to go anywhere they do not want to go and that goes for when they go over their other grandparent's house. I understand that it may be hurtful to her but at the same time she just need to be patient.

Now she is on this me having a baby kick. When I got with her son I told him I could not have any more children and that I didn't want any more and he was cool with it. I guess with him steady having his mama ask for a grandchild he decided that now he wants to have one himself. Which on my end is really not fair at all. I got my tubes tied for a reason and I just thought that he understood that but I guess not. I just get so tired of hearing about me having a baby. I mean sometimes I do think about having another baby but then I look at my children and completely change my mind. I have even thought about adopting a baby but that is just not good enough for him. I love my in-laws but sometimes I just feel like I don't belong in their family. I mean it's not like they make me feel uncomfortable or anything because they don't. I think it's mainly because my husband doesn't deal with them like that. The funny thing is that he is always trying to make me deal with them like they are not his family. I didn't know then but I know now that he doesn't feel like they are his family. Sad I know. He never included himself in any of their family gatherings unless his mama cries or something. I was kind of shock when he did the Christmas photo for his mama. I'm so mad at him because I feel like he kept a whole lot of stuff from me about himself and his family. I feel like they want us in their family but at the same time I feel like they want us to be at a distant also. I'm probably wrong but either way is cool with me, I'm not mad. I wish things were different with my in-laws but with me being afraid of dogs it is kind of impossible because they have dogs and I am uncomfortable around dogs. I just hope they understand that I am not intentionally trying to avoid them it is just I need to first get over my fear of dogs well animals for that matter. It is nothing personal.

Scared to Change

The definition of change is to make or become different, to do something else.

Why is it so hard to accept change? This is what I ask myself on a daily basis when it comes to my family. It's like they expect you to follow some kind of code that they came up with when it comes to living your life. I thought that life was full of choices but with my family the moment you decide you want to do something with your life outside of their norm. To them you are trying to be better than them in some sick ass way and you become the topic of discussion and not in a good way. I don't understand why they would not want for you to be able to live a better life than they had to live or chose to live. They always try to make you feel bad for wanting to live a good and comfortable life. Like you are committing the ultimate sin or something. I remember when I brought my Mac Book. They talked about me so bad because I didn't want anyone messing with it. So I had to inform them on how much I paid for it, why did I do that. I guess only certain people in the family can treat themselves to something nice and expensive and I am not one of those people in their eyes. Yeah right I don't know who mad that law but guess what I am breaking it and will continue to do so.

I use to get upset to the point where I would end up in tears but now I just laugh at them because they are so freaking sad to me. I feel so sorry for them on the real. You would think that with a family as big as mine that we would be all for self-development and pride but this family is just the opposite. They like to see you struggle and be without because in some sick way I guess it makes them feel like they have accomplished something. Over the years I have tried to figure out why they are like that but I have not found any reason some people could be so freaking evil. I don't understand why they don't want to see their family members do something great or good. I am so tired of living my life scared to change just because I don't think they are going to approve what I want to do. If they only knew that my first love was to be a writer they would turn their nose up at me as if I am hopeless and want to do nothing with my life. To me being a writer is very hard work and I love to write because it gives me the opportunity to express myself through words on paper. I have been writing since I was ten years old but no one would know that because they never took the time to ask or to take any interest in what I really wanted to do with my life.

All they think about is how to get over on me. I told them that I wanted to be a lawyer and now they act as if I am about to be a money machine. Talking about they cannot wait because we need a lawyer in the family. I mean that is all good but they have a reason for what they want and trust me it is not a good reason, it's more like a selfish one. I am all for being a lawyer but I also want to be a writer. I remember one time one of my cousins that I don't even know had gotten into some trouble and the first thing they said was "see if you would have hurried up with the lawyer thing then you could've represented your cousin." My response was yeah right when I do become a lawyer I am not representing anyone in my family unless I really want to not because anyone think I should. You can only imagine the look on their faces when I said that but I didn't care. I have come to realize that family can be your worse enemy. I have a long way to go to be a lawyer but in the mean time I am going to try this writing thing until I finish law school and pass the bar exam.

I even want to be a business owner but talking like that within this family is a big no no. My peoples is known for cooking so I came to them with the idea of opening a small little soul food diner but they just looked at me funny. Then someone else in the family said the same thing I said and now all of a sudden they want to do it. The thing is they are just so scared to actually go out there and try. They are more afraid that it is not going to work in their favor, they are afraid of failure. My thing is how do you reach success when you are afraid to take a risk. You never know what you can do until you try. I don't mind taking a risk, I mean if I don't succeed at least I can look back and see what I did wrong so that when I try it again I will know what not to do the next time. When I try to talk to them they just look at me as if I don't know what I am talking about like I am a little kid with big dreams. I do have big dreams and trust me I am going to do all that I can to reach them with or without the support of my family. So now I don't include them in anything I do or think about doing. I mean you cannot be scared all your life.

Blood is Thicker than Water

This is a true and false statement in my eyes. It's true because technically you should not put anyone before your family but sometimes your family can make you feel like you are not apart of the family at all. On another note, you need water in your body to live anyway, lol. I know that the saying does not have anything to do with that but it is a known fact and just a little something I tell myself to put a smile on my face.

I lost my car because I fell behind on my payments trying to get my children into a positive environment. So I had to choose between paying my car note and living in a 4x4 room with 3 children and constantly worry about the fourth one running the streets because they didn't want him in the house. I just got so fed up with that situation that I chose to get my own place instead. Trust me I didn't think that I would get it especially with my credit being the way it is. I went and explained my situation to the rental agent and the next morning he called me and told me that I was approved. He even went down on the rent and let me move in with what I had in my pocket, which was $200. I took it as a blessing from the Man above.

Now that I am without a car I can barely get a ride to and from work from the people in my family. So for the sake of begging and being told no I just ask someone on my job to take me home. It is a damn shame that I have to do that especially when I am out here trying to better myself. As for getting a ride to school that was out of the question. Now I got to find a way to catch up my grades whenever I do get a ride again or fail for the semester. Hopefully that will be sooner than later because I do not want my grades to drop because of this. I have worked too fucking hard to fall behind right now especially when I am scheduled to graduate next May. I have come too damn far. I remember one time my kids grandmother came all the way for Suffolk just to take me to work when my family were only a five-minute walk from me with a vehicle. They always got a reason for not being able to do something for you when you need them. This time they claimed something was wrong with the car. I'm not saying that they were lying but that is what they do to make you feel bad for asking them to do something if they do decide to do it.

But trust me on the first of the month watch how quick my phone ring for me to buy them some food from off of my benefit card. One time I had been asking for a ride to wash my children clothes for over a week. I have had to hand wash my children some towels out so that they will be able to take a bath. It had even gotten to a point when my children had to re-wear some of their clothes because I didn't have a way to cash my check to go wash their clothes. You would think that I was just asking for a ride without offering them gas money but that was not the type of person I was. I always pay my way no matter what. I have to give my god sister props because when she was able to take me she did. Now we are both in the same boat, car-less. Trust me we won't be like this for too long. I am just so tired of bending over backward for my damn family when they are not trying or even acting like they are willing to do the same for me.

It took me a minute but I finally got a vehicle this time without a car note attached to it. I didn't want to add another bill to my list especially with me doing it by myself. I already know that my phone is about to start back ringing again for a ride here and there. Not this time around I am not doing that again because when it came time for me to get a vehicle I had to get it by myself, no one offered me any money towards getting it when they knew damn well they were going to be calling for a ride somewhere. It's okay I don't have a problem playing the fool once maybe even twice but I'll be damn if I play that role for the third time. I mean I have so many people who are willing to help me that are not in my family but I need to do this by myself. I'm not trying to be selfish or anything I just need to do this to gain my independence back, I was a dependent (so to speak) for so long that I almost got comfortable. I cannot do that because it is not me at all. I cannot sit around and let someone control everything and I have no say so, hell nah not this chick! I am trying to teach myself a lesson and that is to depend on no one but self. Trust me I am definitely learning, lol! I just hope that God is proud of the choices I am taking to accomplish his mission to greatness! I believe that is what he really wants for me so that is what I am aiming for.

Clear It Out

This chapter is all about airing out a lot of people in my family and close family that get on my damn nerves. For those of you who did me dirty in the past or present this chapter is for you...

Starting from the top my Nana is like the ringleader of the nation of fucked up individuals. She shows so much favoritism with my niece and nephew that the rest of the kids are like a herd of black sheep's. I feel so bad for them because they are going to grow up with a fucked up ass view of their great-grandmother. She caters to those two like they are gold and then gets mad when somebody doesn't give them something when the rest of the herd of black sheep gets something. It's sad because the kids are already starting to see it and the adults don't make it any better because they call it out around them. Wrong is wrong and right is right. Once again the apple doesn't fall too far from the tree because my mama is just like her mama when it comes to her grandkids also. I had her 1st granddaughter and grandson but if you didn't know that you would think that my sister did. She didn't get close to my oldest daughter until about 2 years ago and my youngest until last year, which is so sad because they are 10½ and 8 now. My daddy is so far gone in the equation that it is pointless to even mention him. He hasn't been a father since I was like 12 years old; drugs took ova him. He is trying to make-up for lost time I will give him that. My uncle Big Shot is just like his mama also. He caters to those he wants to and all of the others just have to kick rocks. The funny part is all three of them (not including my daddy) I just talked about cater to the same 2 kids, my sister oldest and youngest child.

My sistas are another book but I am going to start from the youngest. She is so naive that it saddens me. She has made some poor choices also when it comes to her baby fathers. One of them is ok even though he wasn't at first because of the drama he brought with him. I have to give him credit where credit is due because he always had my sista back no matter what and he always tried to rectify the situations when they came up. The other one is just a whore plain and simple. This nigga too many fucking kids for me personally. He is a cool dude he just, I think, he made some poor choices when choosing the girls he slept with. My sista is so pretty and can have any man she desires I just don't know why she chose the ones she chose but hey that's her life she can live however she feels, I just couldn't do it personally.

Now my other sista is a piece of work. She has always been off the chain. I feel sorry for her because she has taken up both of our parent's traits. She will abandon her responsibility just to go hang out with some nothing ass niggas and bitches. She had a so-called good man on her side but she really didn't want him because he cared about her kids and her some of her family liked him. Crazy I know because if he didn't think twice about her kids she would be in love with him but that is my sista. I really believe my sista has low self-esteem she has all of the signs of it. She is out here messing with these men who she doesn't even know and she is a sucker for love even after a conversation, which is sad I know. She never wanted to be a mother on the real. She doesn't even act like one. If she was given the opportunity to get rid of them and live her life trust me she will do it in a fucking minute. You would think that after losing one child that she would straighten up and fly right but hell nah not her. She loves to club and fight too much. I swear she is always getting into something or getting involved in shit that don't have a fucking thing to do with her. Then she says the dumbness shit like "I don't give a fuck!" I just be like she can't be serious she must forgot she got 6 kids that she is responsible for. But when she gets mad she doesn't think about them like a real mother would. Now she got a second chance with another so-called good man but this time some people in her family do not like him, which is causing her to distant herself from him. I think she just need to follow her heart and stop worrying about what these people in this damn family think besides it is her life at the end of the day anyway.

I had a brother whom I don't know too much about because he was

Murdered after us only meeting 6 or 8 months before. He has a little girl who will never know this side of her family because her simple ass mama is just like that. I don't know if I have any other siblings out there even though I was told my daddy had two other daughters but that has yet to be confirmed.

As for my god sistas, one is so naive and dumb as hell. She had this one lil fling that she had been fucking with for years that I felt she needed to let go. She was not benefitting at all from his ass. Not to mention he is a fucking whore who tries to run her life and she somewhat allows him to do so. I don't see how she allows a man who is not her man even suggest anything as far as her life goes. She somehow mistakes her role as his bitch on the side to his main bitch, which is someone she will never be. He doesn't do a damn thing for her but give her a wet ass. She really needs to get her fucking priorities in order and grow the fuck up. The way I see it is if she likes looking stupid then I love looking at her stupid ass, lol! The other has came a long ass way and I am so proud of her. She use to have me worried though because she was just as dumb. Her main problem was that she didn't know how to say "No" and that she likes to take care of men. Fuck that it should be 50/50. She would come in contact with these men who would find that out and start taking advantage of her. I'm glad she finally listened and starting thinking of her first and them niggas last. One thing for sure about all my sisters, I will be damn if I allow another man use either one of them again or even act like they want to bring any harm their way!

My other n-laws the Lang's are special to me only because I have known them for so long and I consider them my real family. Sometimes I don't agree with Mama Naomi but I do listen because she does speak the truth at times even when I don't want to hear it. It would've been 11 years this year if I had stayed with her son but I had to let that go even though I really didn't want to and somewhat still feel like I haven't fully. Nana Pearl is so sweet and has always been every since I met her. Auntie Jazzy is like my home girl. We have had our differences but in the end that is my ace. She knows more about her nephew and me than his mama does. I can talk to her about anything from her nephew to my life in general. They love all of my children equally and that is really why I love and respect them so much. Mama Naomi will always be my mother in law no matter what her son does with himself. Da Lang's have their flaws too. Especially Mama Naomi we have really had our differences. I know more shit about her son than she does and if I was to tell her she wouldn't believe me so I don't. Just like she thinks her son doesn't hit on women sorry boo he does. I remember when he came home after doing a bid we got into it on the real. We were riding in the car with some people he knew. I think he was trying to show off because he started tripping and hitting on me all because I had another baby. He acted as if he was so perfect and never cheated on me when he was cheating on me the whole time and I only stepped out on him once.

As for my new in-laws the Jackson's they are good peoples too. My mama-n-law Shelly is so sweet even though we have had our differences as well but I know she means well so you got to love her! Lol! My sista-n-law Jennifer is cool. I don't really know her like that even though I would like to get to know her I just don't think we would hit it off like I hope. We do however like some of the same things except for her love for dogs, lol! I am scared of them, which is the main reason I do not come around. My brother-n-law Tony is cool too he is like the brother I wish I had outside of my own brother. I just feel sorry for my husband because he doesn't have the type of bond I have with my sistas with his siblings. He says it is due to their age difference but I don't buy it. My husband is the kind of man who likes to showboat all the time. Being braggarific about shit he know damn well he doesn't have. He has even lied to me about petty shit that I be like what the fuck did you lie about something like that for? Some of the shit I know, he has no idea I know about. The Jackson's have their flaws also. Mama Shelly is the kind of person who tries to make you feel bad about certain shit. Just like one time I went ova her house and she asked me if I was hungry and I was like "nah I'm good I don't eat like that." She got offended and I was like I am not going to eat just to make anybody feel good. I am not the type of person who sits around thinking about food all the time but she couldn't understand that. Everyone who knows me knows that I barely eat and when I do I don't eat that much. I just don't have an appetite like that, I never did.

There was another time when her son, my husband, need his tooth pulled. I still believe she was mad because I didn't add him on my insurance. I mean we couldn't afford to add him especially since we were not making that much money and had bills out the ass all ready. Besides he should've had his own damn insurance. As for her relationship with her son that shit is all screwed up. I still have some belief that he was only with me in the beginning to get out of her house because she didn't want him there. I felt like I was his way out and he was mine. One time he told me how they moved and didn't even tell him. They even left all of his stuff at the old place to me that was fucked up. There was another time when he got into a car accident with their car and all her and her husband did was fuss at him. They didn't even bother to see if he was ok. He had fucked his back up and it still gives him problem now. I think he has some built up animosity toward his mama and step daddy along with his biological daddy. I feel so sorry for my husband because he always felt like a black sheep in his family and I think he still feels that way. I am mad because I didn't find out all of this until after we got married. I mean I don't know if I would've been so quick to get married right then well not until he had gotten some counseling. Now he makes me feel bad telling me that I am all he has which is crazy because we haven't been seeing eye to eye here lately.

Overcoming

Living my life and loving it is all I have to do and say for now! I had to come up with a plan to get back on track and I believe it is going to work in my favor this time especially if I stick to it which I plan on doing. I am done with all the bull shit these phony ass people in my family and society have to offer that it is not funny. If it is not about my children and me then fuck it because I don't have all year to wait on the rest of the world to grow the fuck up you know I am not getting any younger. I don't want to live my days wondering what the rest of my life would have been like if I had done things differently you know. Shit I do that now. I like to have fun and enjoy myself. I love going out dancing and being the center of attention. I mean what is wrong with that as long as you are not being reckless? Nothing, I mean if you got it you got it if not try to get it and get with the program. I am changing yall being better than I already am and have been. I am not just doing this for me but for my children as well. The new me is not putting up with a bunch of nonsense any more. I use to sit up at night crying about all of the foolishness my family use to put me through and all of the mistakes I have made in my life. I'm done with all that now life is too short. You can say I got my swagga back, Lol!

Thanks to my kids, their fathers, my husband, my friends, and my family I have come to see things more clearly. All these years I thought I was not worthy of greatness and some of ya led me to believe that shit but no more. I am back and in full effect! I can feel myself overcoming all of this bullshit I have been subjected to for so long and it feels wonderful. I just hope that some of the people in my family wake the fuck and see that this is a new day and we are all offered the same thing I just chose to use mine so stop hating on me. I mean look in the white house; we got a Black (well mixed) President for goodness sake. I'm done starving for attention and acceptance from my family. If you don't see me now trust you are going to want to see me later. Now I don't give a fuck if they accept me or not. I am tired of losing sleep ova people who are not losing any ova me. I am proud of myself for not falling subject to my family hateful and racist ways because little do my family know every white person is not racist, try looking at yourself for once. Disliking someone because of what they are or the color of their skin is a form of racism, which is how my family is so what makes them any better. I feel sorry for my family for real because of the shit they had to experience to cause them to have a cold heart against other races. My husband is Spanish, Filipino, Indian, and Black but the only reason they even somewhat accept him is because he looks like he is black with good hair. In the beginning they loved him that was until we moved in together and got married then they did a complete 360 they act as if he is the worse man in the world or the worse man I have ever dealt with when really he is a wonderful man he just have some issues.

My family was not the only one to change because he did also. He basically went into his own little world and left me out but to be honest I really didn't want to be in that world because he was not the same there and I didn't want any parts of it. It's like he was a complete stranger. I mean I stop wearing my wedding ring and all because I don't know where my husband went or if I was really married at all. I know that sounds crazy but that is how I really felt. I know I have changed but I'm just mad that he didn't change with me that is why I feel we have grown apart. I wanted and still do want certain things in life that I don't think he wants or at least he doesn't show any interest in. I do feel like he kept a lot of stuff from me about himself and honestly that was not fair to me. Some stuff I really didn't care about but I still feel like he could've at least warned me about some of the other things he was dealing with. At least then I would've known how to take him and our marriage would probably still be going strong.

As for myself I still have a lot of self re-assurance to do but for now I'm good. I know I haven't really overcome it all and there are still a lot more things that I need to work on but for now I have overcame a whole lot and that should count for something. I am so proud of myself for all that I have overcome. With the Man upstairs help I will continue to climb to the top. Negative people and surroundings are no longer allowed in my circuit. I'm done with that part of my life. So if you are not with me then you must be against me, but it is all good either way for now! I have now realized that blood don't make us family!

Everyone loves a star when she's on the top
But no one ever comes around when she starts to drop!

~~~

Family Ties

They say the family that prays together stays together and that
blood is thicker than water
But if the blind is leading the blind it's like wolves in sheep
clothing leading the lambs to the slaughter
Gone are the days of each one teach one everyone is out for
themselves there's got to be a heaven because I'm living in hell
You pray on my downfall rather than see me prevail is it because
your body is free but your mind is trapped in a cell
Or maybe you don't want me to succeed where you failed
I held it in long enough I've finally exhaled!

Envious

Acknowledgements

Acknowledgments

I am a young Black Woman who has been through a lot in my life and is still standing tall. My Children (Quintelle, Marquezia, Shyderia, and Quadeyr) you all give me the will power and a reason to do what I am doing. I Love you all so very much with all of my heart and soul! You guys mean the world to me! You all are my inspiration, determination, and my reason for doing what I am doing now. Without them none of what I am going to go through will be possible because they keep me going and wanting more and I hope I do the same for them.

I want to give thanks to the Man above for helping me find my way back to myself and for never leaving my side when I thought you did. To my dysfunctional family for all the negative energy that could've shattered my dreams but instead I used it as steam to power my dreams.

To my extended family the Young's thanks for always keeping it 100 with me no matter what, Mama Pam, Grandma Paulette,

Aunt Sharon, and Anthony I love you all! Also the Keene's who also kept it real with me: Mr. Rick, Mrs. Sarah, Jessica, John, and Damien I love ya too. My in-laws The Jansak's, thanks for also giving a helping hand when I needed it. Mama Merlie, Marylynn, and Juni I love guys also.

Last but definitely not least I want to say thank you to my main family the Sanderson's, Davis's, Smith's and Dozier's! It is too many of ya to mention so I am only going to mention a few but for those I didn't mention please don't take it personal yah know we got a HUGE family! Nana thanks for all that you did teach me whether it was negative or positive because I chose my own road to follow, I Love You Old Lady! Mama I envy you the most because you really are a beautiful strong black woman you just don't know it yet and I hope you figure it out soon. I love you too! Daddy thanks for what you tried to teach me even though you were too late and thanks for never beating me because if you didn't know that made me who I am today and the reason I would never allow a man to put his hands on me, I love ya!

My real sisters (Teea and Crystal) and god sisters (LaTia and Shavon) you all are my aces no matter what even though you all piss me off at times but I still love you all very much! My 6 nephews and 4 nieces auntie loves ya!

I have a wonderful partner who tries to support me in every

way possible. He is wonderful because I know at times I can be unbearable and stubborn and he still puts up with me. That says a lot about him. You are my inspiration to this whole thing and I really want to thank you for all of your support. I Love Ya! .

This is to some special people in my circle; ya know I had to send ya some shout outs! Davida and Alicia ya are my girls 100 grand I love you like sisters, Jasmine my somewhat adopted daughter that somehow won't leave even though we don't have any papers on her, and Mikey the funniest man I know when I need to laugh I know who I can always call on.

I want to give a R.I.P. to my Papa Leon I know if you were still alive this family would be back in order I miss you so much, my niece Alysse you was such a good baby never a crybaby I didn't then but I do now understand why God felt the need to take you home with him because you was truly an Angel, my brother Brandon I miss talking to you and your smile looking just like daddy. I know you hated to hear that. I love you bro! You all may be gone but you will never be forgotten.

*** Be on the look out for some more of my work coming real soon. Ladies and single mothers I definitely got some stuff you are going to want to check out!

www.ingramcontent.com/pod-product-compliance
Lightning Source LLC
LaVergne TN
LVHW011214080426
835508LV00007B/778